PET OWNER'S GUIDE TO THE
WEIMARANER

Gillian Averis BVMS, MRCVS

RINGPRESS

ABOUT THE AUTHOR

Gillian Averis BVMS, MRCVS is a practising veterinary surgeon who has been involved with gundogs all her life. She breeds Weimaraners under her Sireva affix, and has enjoyed considerable success in the show ring. Awarded the Top Breeder award, Gillian has bred numerous Show Champions, and Weimaraners from her kennel have been awarded Top Dog, Top Brood Bitch, and Top Puppy titles. Two home-bred Weimaraners also won Best Bitch at Crufts.

Gillian, who judged Weimaraners at Crufts in 1999, is also interested in the working side of the breed. Several of her dogs are trained to work during the shooting season. She lives in Yorkshire with her group of 20 Weimaraners, plus Sussex Spaniels, German Shorthaired Pointers and Labrador Retrievers.

Photography: Keith Allison

Published by Ringpress Books,
Vincent Lane, Dorking, Surrey,
RH4 3YX, England.

First published 2000
© Interpet Publishing. All rights reserved

ISBN 1 86054 181 X

Printed and bound in Hong Kong by Printworks International Ltd.

CONTENTS

1 Introducing The Weimaraner

The Weimaraner is a member of the Hunt Point Retrieve (HPR) sub-group of Gundogs. As the name suggests, these dogs come from Weimar, an area in Eastern Germany. The exact origins of this wonderful breed are not clearly known, and many theories exist, but whichever breeds were used in its foundation, they created a wonderful dog – aristocratic in appearance, a superior gundog and a protective family dog.

ORIGINS

It is believed that the founding father of the Weimaraner was Grand Duke Karl August, who may have shot over a grey lithe dog and brought some back with him to Weimar, where they were developed into the Weimaraner. The St. Hubert Bracken seems to be a strong contender for Weimaraner ancestor, with theories about the introduction of the Great Dane, Pointing dog, and, less likely, the German Shorthaired Pointer.

From this early development by the Grand Duke and the noblemen of Weimar, our modern dog was created. In 1631, Van Dyck painted a portrait of Prince Rupprecht von der Pfalz with his favourite hunting dog – silver-grey in colour, with pendent ears and an undocked tail – most likely, one of the dogs from which the Grand Duke developed the breed.

As hunting methods changed, the dogs had to change as well. Bird dogs had to range ahead of the guns, and, when they scented game, they would stand immobile (pointing) while the gunmen came within range. The quarry could be flushed, shot by the hunters and then retrieved by these versatile dogs. The Weimaraner was bred as a superb hunting dog, strong in body and with good stamina. The ground around Weimar was

Weimaraners were bred to be brave and strong, with great powers of endurance.

populated with an abundance of game, so a dog that could find the quarry was needed – hence the need for a strong scenting ability. Weimaraners were expected to hunt many sorts of game, from rabbits and birds to wild boar, and so they had to be brave, strong and with plenty of endurance. These attributes are still found in our modern-day Weimaraners, whether they are family pets, guards or shooting companions.

In 1896, the Delegate Commission of Germany finally accepted the Weimaraner as a separate breed. The following year,

a Breed Standard was formed. Several people in Germany and, latterly, Austria, were very influential in the development of the Weimaraner. Early in the 20th century, Major Robert Herber earned himself the title of Father of the Weimaraners – he was very influential in the breed's development. In 1921, he became president of the German Weimaraner Club. Major Herber's close friend, von Otto, was a dog show judge, and, along with Dr Paul Kleemann, they encouraged the development of the breed in Germany. The early Austrian authority was Prince Hans von Ratibor, who formed an Austrian Club and was extremely important to the breed's development in his country.

WEIMARANERS IN THE UK

Two army officers who had seen Weimaraners working while on tour in Germany decided to try to acquire some of these Grey Ghosts. Major Bob Petty and Colonel Richardson were stationed in West Germany, but not far from the border with East Germany and the region of Weimar. They managed to find someone who knew someone else in the Eastern zone, and, in total, 13 Weimaraners were acquired. All these were finally brought back to England in 1952. At a similar time, Mrs Olga Malet, returning after a tour of duty with the Air Force, also brought a pair into the UK. Out of these dogs, only nine were thought to be of good enough quality to breed from, so they were registered with the Kennel Club in the United Kingdom and formed the foundation stock of all the Weimaraners in the UK. With interest growing in Weimaraners, Major Petty instigated the foundation of the Weimaraner

Club of Great Britain, and, by 1953, the Weimaraner had arrived on the UK dog scene.

When news of the importation and release from quarantine of these unusually coloured dogs became known to the press, a reporter wrote an article that caused the breed many problems in its early years in the UK. He wrote a story reporting that these

The 'grey ghosts' were soon highly prized as companion dogs.

dogs were smuggled from East Germany; he painted them as wonder dogs and stressed their value. This immediately encouraged some people to buy Weimaraners to breed from them for the money, with no interest in the development of the breed. This exploitation slowed down its development in Britain.

The Weimaraner first made its appearance at Crufts in 1953. As there were no classes exclusively for Weimaraners, they had to be exhibited in Any Variety Gundog classes. There were 12 entered. Two years later, in 1955, Crufts granted Weimaraners their own separate classes. From an entry of just 18 in 1955, the entry has grown to 255 in 1998! The early Weimaraners were not only shown, but were also campaigned in Field Trials by Major Petty. They had to compete against either Setters or Retrievers, as there were no Trials at that time for HPRs. This was a tremendous disadvantage, as the versatile all-round gundog can never compete at the highest standard with specialists.

Several years later, special trials for HPRs were organised by the newly-formed German Shorthaired Pointer Club, but it was not until 1967 that the Weimaraner won a first at a Novice Trial. In the show scene, the Kennel Club awarded Challenge Certificates (CCs) for the breed for the first time in 1960. This allowed the crowning of the first Show Champion (Sh. Ch.). The breed did not have long to wait, with the first one being the bitch Sh. Ch. Wolfox Silverglance. The second Show Champion, Sh. Ch. Strawbridge Oliver, followed shortly afterwards, and he then became the first Champion (Ch.) when he qualified in 1961 at a GSP Field Trial.

WEIMARANERS IN THE USA

Weimaraners were exported to America in 1929, some 23 years before they came to the United Kingdom. An enthusiastic sportsman, Howard Knight was unable to breed from his dogs as they were sterile, but, after confirming his opinion of these wonderful dogs as outstanding all-round gundogs, he managed to bring five more into the USA in 1938. These provided the basis for the American Weimaraner. The Weimaraner is a very popular gundog in America, used as a family pet, shooting companion and successful show dog. The Weimaraner has also made his mark in most parts of the world, from Hawaii and Canada to Australia and New Zealand.

The first Weimaraner club in America was formed in 1941. Weimaraners made their first show appearance in America in 1943 following recognition from the American Kennel Club.

The versatile Weimaraner is still widely used as a working gundog.

2 Choosing A Weimaraner

When you have decided you would like a Weimaraner, stop and make sure you are in a position to give him the sort of life he needs.

As with all breeds of dog, the basic requirement should be that he will not be left at home from nine to five, with no human contact. Another consideration is whether you have an enclosed area of garden for quick toilet breaks. It may seem okay to go for a late-night walk around the block, but this is not so appealing on a freezing, wet winter night. You do not need a huge garden; not many are big enough to provide sufficient exercise or stimulation for a Weimaraner, so a small, confined area would be suitable, and then he can obtain his exercise on long daily walks. The third, and most important, criterion is that you can provide a home for a Weimaraner for the next 12 years or more. It cannot be a whim of

fashion. The dog you choose will, hopefully, be part of the family for the next decade; he cannot be disregarded because your circumstances change. You need to think what the future might hold. Do you plan to have a family? Will you be moving abroad? If you are happy that you can provide a permanent home for a dog, then look closely at the Weimaraner temperament.

TEMPERAMENT

The Weimaraner is a member of the Hunt Point Retrieve sub-group of Gundogs. Being a gundog, his temperament is friendly and biddable, but he is an intelligent, determined and dominant dog. You need to be more intelligent and determined than he is, and, if you are, then you will have a wonderful addition to your family. However, he will soon catch on if you do not mean what you say, and he

will push until he has the upper hand. You will then own a 'nuisance'.

The Weimaraner is very protective of his home and owners. This can be reassuring, because he will protect you if you are threatened, but it is important that you do not encourage this side of the Weimaraner character. He will protect you when necessary without any special training. My first Weimaraner, Emma, was a big softy. I often wondered whether she would protect me if I was ever threatened, but I was not sure. One weekend I was staying at my sister's house, sleeping with Emma at my side. My brother-in-law, whom she knew, came into the room and told me to get up. As a joke, he grabbed the bottom of the sleeping bag and began to pull. I shouted out in protest and Emma, thinking I was being attacked, jumped up and stood right up to my brother-in-law, telling him that now she meant business if he stepped any closer. At this point he told me to go back to sleep and slunk out! It was not a real attack, but it did make me realise that I was in safe hands when Emma was about.

Weimaraners are good family pets and are fine with children, as long as children are okay with them. They should be taught that a dog is not a toy to be picked up, poked, pestered or played with too roughly. They have to learn that the dog is a living being, and should be respected. If pushed too hard, the dog's only way to retaliate is to bite, and he will then be to blame.

A Weimaraner wants to be part of the family, not locked away in a kennel or in an empty room. He will sit with a foot on yours, just to make sure you cannot sneak off without him! He is a good traveller and will enjoy driving around with you. A short period of isolation in a kennel is all right, but the majority of a Weimaraner's time should be spent with humans.

DOG OR BITCH?

Should you have a dog or a bitch? I have my favourites of both sexes, and it is really a personal choice. Bitches are less dominant and can be easier for a first-time owner. The problem with them is that they have seasons, but that can be rectified by spaying, if you do not want to breed from yours.

Males are more dominant and generally bigger, but, because of

Children and Weimaraners get along fine, as long as they learn a sense of respect for each other.

that, they have more character and are certainly impressive animals. However, they can be more of a challenge. The breeder may be able to give you some advice, having seen you and heard about your circumstances.

PUPPY OR ADULT?

You may decide that you would rather have an older dog than a puppy. There are always older dogs in Weimaraner Rescue

Societies. It can be a good idea to give one a home, but do make sure you are not taking on someone else's problem – you should find out why the dog needs rehoming. It might be that a couple have split up and can no longer provide a home, but it may be that the dog has had no training and will need re-educating, and quite a lot of patience. A rescue dog can be an excellent choice, but do think seriously first.

HOW MANY PUPPIES?

I will never sell two puppies to one person at the same time. Two is not just double trouble, it can be worse than that. They will egg each other on, and they are difficult to train. It is much easier to leave them together than to do a bit of training. They tend to bond with each other, rather than with you. It is a much better idea, if you want more than one, to leave at least nine months between puppies. You will then have trained the first one, and he will train the younger puppy, making your job much easier.

FINDING A BREEDER

There are several ways of finding a suitable puppy. Your best option is

The male Weimaraner (right) is bigger, and can be more dominant than the female.

to go to a well-known and recognised breeder who has a deep knowledge of the breed. Your national Kennel Club should be able to put you in touch with either breeders or the Breed Club societies. We are fortunate in that the Weimaraner breed has not been split into 'show' and 'working' dogs as yet, but, if you are seriously considering one or the other, it would be sensible to go to a kennel that has proved that their stock is capable of being successful in that field. It is worth taking the kennel's claims of success with a pinch of salt – some look at their dogs through rose-tinted glasses.

Go to some Championship shows and look at the dogs – you might see a few that you really like. If you are lucky, they may have been bred by the same kennel, or sired by the same stud dog. This makes your choice of

Make sure you go to a recognised and respected breeder.

where to go much easier. The top winning kennel might not have the dog for you – you have to live with the Weimaraner for the next 12 years. If you do not like that kennel's dogs – it may be the shade of colour, the head shape, the temperament, or something else – then there is no point in having a dog from them. He might be a show winner, but how many shows are there in a year? The rest of the time, you will have to live with him!

If you want a dog to shoot over or to trial, then it would be sensible to ask if that kennel has experience in either field. However, much of a dog's working capabilities result from how he is raised, trained and what experience he has, so it is not essential that a shooting companion should come from parents that are worked.

You may decide that all you want is a family companion and pet. I would still recommend that

there and then; but that is unlikely. You may well have to wait a considerable time for a puppy. The wait is worth it, as a poorly-bred puppy is still going to be with you for 12 years or so, and may cause you a lot of heartache if he is not healthy. Do not rush to buy the first puppy that you can find. Buying a Weimaraner is not the same as buying a new car. They are not all the same. A knowledgeable breeder will have researched the parents of a planned litter carefully, having a deep knowledge of the breed's needs, problems and faults. They might well have travelled to the other end of the country to use the stud dog they want, rather than a pet dog down the road just because he was convenient.

MEETING THE BREEDER

When you first contact the breeder, you should expect an interrogation to see if you are a suitable person to own a Weimaraner. Do not be offended when the breeder asks you about your circumstances. Do you work? Who will be with the puppy? Do you have children? Do you expect children? Do you have a safe garden? Do you know anything about the breed? If you are not

you go to a recognised and respected breeder. Show dogs have to mix well with other dogs, and, most importantly for a pet, should have a good temperament. This is essential because the show dog must allow a stranger (the judge) to look in his mouth and to feel him all over. This same temperament is what you need in family pet.

Having decided on a kennel, you might strike lucky in that the breeder may have a litter available asked such questions, it may be that the breeder only wants you to part with your money, and is not bothered where the puppies go, just as long as they go.

A reputable breeder will give you the good and bad points about owning a Weimaraner, and will take the puppy back if, at any time in the future, you cannot give the dog a home. If the breeder of the litter is satisfied with you, they will invite you to see their dogs. It is useful if you can see several generations, but this is not essential.

Weimaraners are not a fussy breed and will usually greet you with a few woofs, check you over and then settle back down. They are not overfussy with strangers, but will watch you closely and jump up quickly if anything interesting appears to be happening. This is a good time to check that no member of your family is allergic to Weimaraners. If you can all spend a short time in an enclosed space with a few dogs, it should give you a good idea whether there will be any problems. It is unusual for people to be allergic to Weimaraners because they do not have a dense coat, but it is as well to check before you buy a puppy rather than

to risk the heartache of having to return him to his breeder.

ASSESSING THE PUPPIES
Once the breeder is happy with you, they will show you any puppies that are available. If the bitch is with the puppies, she may be protective towards them, so do not rush up too quickly. She may perceive you as a threat to her puppies and guard them, so just let her get used to you first. Only when the bitch is happy, and when the breeder says it is okay, should you touch the puppies.

Depending on the age of the puppies, you may be able to choose your dog. There is little point before they are six weeks old, as their characters will not have started to develop, and, if there are any that are going to show homes, they will be selected at about that time.

Many people say that they want to show, thinking that they will get the best puppy. The best puppy to show might not be the best puppy for you, if you just want a family pet.

Take the advice of your breeder. The show dog may not make the best Agility dog, worker or family pet. Be honest about what you are looking for.

Weimaraner puppies are hugely appealing, but take time to assess the litter before making your choice.

If you are looking for a puppy to work as a gundog, you still want a well-made dog, with good bone and a substantial body, because he will have to be capable of hunting and retrieving game for long periods. You should also look for the inquisitive puppy who wants to bring things to you.

An Agility dog needs to be quick on his legs and biddable, wanting to please you. A smaller-framed puppy may find the weaving poles easier than a hefty dog. A companion dog needs the character to suit you. Often, it is the middle-of-the-road character that you need, not the one that rushes up or the one that sits at the back of the box.

CHOOSING A SHOW PROSPECT

If you really want to show and the breeder has been successful in the show ring, then ask their advice on which one is most likely to be the best. If the breeder is not an experienced show person, take someone with you who is used to assessing show potential in Weimaraner puppies. Potential is all there is in a puppy – the best puppy in the litter can usually be found, but there is no guarantee that he will go on to be a winner. You buy a pet puppy that *might* grow into a show dog. The best time to choose a puppy for show is at about six to eight weeks old. I watch the puppies playing and walking around, to check that they move properly. Their front legs should move in a straight line in front of them, with toes turning neither in nor out. Similarly, the back legs should move straight out behind the dog. The front and back legs should move on the same tracks when walking.

Once I have checked that I am happy with the movement, I stand the puppy up in a show pose on a table. If the surface is slippery, I put a rubber mat or piece of bedding on the top to stop the puppy slipping, and it gives him confidence. I like to put a mirror on a wall behind the puppy so that I can look at his outline. You cannot describe easily what to look for, but I want a flowing picture of a miniature Weimaraner. That is, medium-length neck, well-constructed front and rear legs, and a good long ribcage. After that, I will check to see that his feet are well arched, and that he has a good forechest and a pleasing expression.

If I had two puppies of equal merit, I would then look at their colour. Out of choice, I would prefer a silver-grey colour to a darker grey, but colour is not everything – good conformation is as important. The 'ideal' dog is described in the Breed Standard – the blueprint for the breed as accepted by the Kennel Club. The UK and USA Breed Standards are similar, with a few important differences. The main difference is that the longhaired variety is not recognised by the American Kennel Club – in fact, it is a disqualifying fault.

THE IDEAL DOG

The dog's hunting ability should be the most important concern when assessing a dog. When a judge is looking at a Weimaraner in a show ring, it is difficult to assess this, but he is looking for a dog that looks like he could work if he was out on a shoot. If the construction of the dog is correct, he should be able to work. He should appear to be keen, fearless and friendly, protective and obedient.

He is a medium-sized grey dog.

*At 12 weeks of age, this
puppy looks promising.*

*The same bitch, now
a Show Champion.*

Pictured left: The great honour of winning the Best Bitch at Crufts.

The colour is described as preferably silver-grey, but shades of mouse-grey or roe-grey are acceptable. The AKC Standard does not specify any particular shades of grey. There is often a lighter band on the head and ears, and, occasionally, a darker stripe down the back. It is important that this unique colour is preserved, as it is a very distinctive feature of the Weimaraner. The coat should give the appearance of metallic sheen, and a small white mark is allowed on the chest. He should look balanced, alert, and appear to have great driving force – that is, well-muscled hindquarters. He should be able to cover the ground effortlessly and smoothly with long strides. When seen from the rear, the hind feet should parallel the front feet.

The Standard asks for moderation in the Weimaraner – moderate height, moderate stop, moderate angulation, moderate neck, etc. He is not a dog of exaggeration.

HEAD

The Weimaraner is an aristocratic dog, and his head should give this impression – looking down his nose at you. His head is moderately long, with only a moderate stop (the area between the eyes). The length of the foreface should be the same as the length from the stop to the back of the head. This gives the head a balanced look and an aristocratic appearance.

The Weimaraner's ears are particularly long for a gundog. When gently pulled forward, they should reach within one inch of the tip of the nose. They are long and lobular, with a slight fold. The eyes are unusual in the dog world; they are medium-sized and light-coloured in shades of blue-grey to amber. As a young puppy, the Weimaraner's eyes are a beautiful shade of pale blue. As he gets older, his eyes tend to become more amber-coloured.

BODY

The neck is moderately long with a slight arch. The forelegs are straight and strong when viewed from the front. The shoulder blade should be well laid and sloping backwards to form a near right angle with the upper arm. The upper arm should be long, and these features allow the dog to reach forward in a long, ground-covering stride. The measurement from the top of the shoulder to the elbow should equal the

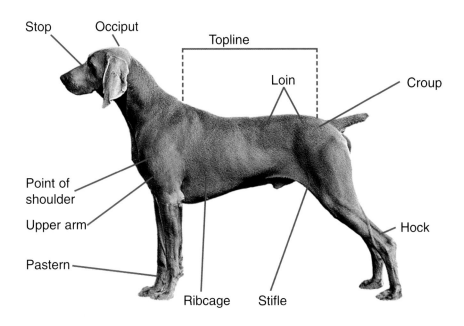

Stop   Occiput   Topline   Loin   Croup
Point of shoulder   Upper arm   Pastern   Ribcage   Stifle   Hock

measurement from the elbow to the ground. The body is long – not square, like many gundogs. The length from the withers to the base of the tail is the same as from the withers to the ground. This might seem to make the Weimaraner square, but the forechest in front of the withers makes the body shape oblong. The Weimaraner needs a deep ribcage and long ribs to give him plenty of lung room, allowing him to breathe in lots of energy-giving oxygen. The topline is level, with a slight slope over the hips to the tail, and the abdomen is moderately tucked-up but held

firmly. In the AKC Standard, the back is described as of moderate length and slightly sloping from the withers to the croup – very different from the long back and level topline of the UK Standard.

The hindquarters propel the dog forward, so they have to be moderately angulated with good muscle tone in the UK. The USA Standard calls for the hindquarters to be well angulated.

FEET
The Weimaraner needs to have firm, compact, arched and well-padded feet to prevent him from damaging his joints when landing

heavily. The arching toes and pads help to absorb concussion and to decrease wear to the joint surfaces. The tail is customarily docked, except in the longhaired variety, where only the tip is removed.

MOVEMENT

To enable the Weimaraner to hunt all day long, he has to move in an efficient, ground-covering, easy stride. If he has the right body shape and firm muscle, he will be able to do this. This build will also allow him to run and play all day long as a family pet.

SIZE

The size of the Weimaraner is taken from the withers, and should be 22 to 25 ins (56 to 63.5 cms) for bitches and 24 to 27 ins (61 to 68.5 cms) for dogs. However, there are variations, but

The longhaired Weimaraner is still limited in numbers.

a Weimaraner who is too big is not desirable, as he will struggle to do a full day's work because of the strain on his bones and muscles. On the other hand, one that is too small will not have enough stamina. In the USA, the range is more restrictive – the lower height for both sexes is one inch higher than in the UK.

THE LONGHAIRED WEIMARANER

The vast majority of Weimaraners have a short, smooth and sleek coat, but there is a longhaired variety. As well as being the product of two longhaired dogs, this rare coat type can occur when two shorthaired dogs that both carry the recessive gene for long hair are mated together. In the longhaired, the coat is 1 to 2 ins (2.5 to 5 cms) long on the body, with longer hairs on the neck, chest, belly, tail and the back of the legs. The first to appear in the UK was a litter which was born in Scotland. Since then, several have been imported from Austria and Germany to try to establish the longhaired variety in the UK, but their number is still limited. At dog shows, the longhaired is exhibited in the same classes as the more numerous shorthaired variety. This has probably not been to the advantage of the longhaired, as they are very much the odd ones out – usually, there are only one or two in an entry of 160. Despite this handicap, two dogs have become Show Champions, with several others obtaining high awards.

The coat of the longhaired needs regular grooming to keep it in good condition and tangle-free. A soft brush should be used first, and then a metal comb or slicker brush on the feathering – but be careful not to catch the skin; just groom the coat.

LEAVING THE LITTER

Having chosen the puppy, ask the breeder at what age he can leave his littermates. You will probably have to wait until your puppy is about eight weeks old before you can bring him home. He will have been weaned from his mother at about five weeks, but I feel it is important that puppies learn to play together within the litter, so that they begin to learn 'doggy' behaviour. If they play too roughly, they will be told off by their littermates – it is an all-important part of learning dog body language.

3 *The Weimaraner Puppy*

Y ou can start preparing for the new addition to your family before you collect your puppy.

EQUIPMENT

FEEDING BOWLS: You will need two feeding bowls – one for water and one for food. I find the stainless steel ones are the best, as they are less easily chewed and are easily cleaned.

Collars And Leads: All dogs must wear collars and identification when outside. When you first get your puppy, it may be as well to get a material puppy collar, which can be enlarged as the puppy grows. They grow so quickly that they can soon outgrow a collar, so check it regularly. I prefer the half-check collar. This is part leather or material and part chain. It can be worn all the time, but has a semi-choke chain action, which gives you more control than an ordinary collar.

The best type of lead is a three-quarter inch (2 cm) wide leather or nylon one. This will not dig into your hand like a chain will when you are training.

You should walk your dog on a loose lead, and only pull the lead back in a quick movement and then release the pressure.

Toys: Toys need to be selected carefully. I would strongly recommend that you do not buy any squeaky toys – the incessant noise will soon drive you mad. They can also encourage your dog to mouth birds, if he is going on to be used as a gundog. There are some excellent toys produced by well-known manufacturers that are safe for your puppy, and will help to keep him amused.

I often use plastic bottles (with the tops removed). They are cheap, will not damage the house when thrown around and make a great noise when the dog picks them up.

You can start making preparations before your puppy arrives home.

Once they start to be chewed, I remove them and supply a new one.

There are some specially designed toys that can help keep canine teeth and gums healthy – your vet can advise you on these. They are worth investing in because dental disease is a big problem for many dogs.

Be very careful what type of ball you use. It is quite easy, when a dog jumps up and catches a ball, for it then to lodge in the windpipe and suffocate the dog, so do make sure the ball is bigger than a tennis ball for an adult Weimaraner. Sticks can be dangerous too. If you throw one and it stands end-on in the ground, the dog may run on to the stick and it could become impaled in the back of the mouth, causing a nasty injury requiring surgical treatment. Frisbees are excellent toys, as they can be thrown long distances and are relatively safe.

Beds: You will need somewhere cosy for your puppy to sleep. Initially, a cardboard box is good, because you can change it as he chews it or grows out of it! As your puppy grows older, you may like to buy him a proper bed. The traditional wicker basket is not a good idea, as they are easily chewed, collect the dust and are not easy to wash and to keep clean. Plastic beds are great, as the sides are deep, making your dog draught-free and secure. There are some now with ventilation in the bottom, which prevents the bed from becoming damp. There are numerous other material beds, duvets or beanbags etc., which can provide a soft comfortable place to sleep. Beware of beanbags. If your dog chews one, you will get polystyrene beads everywhere!

I like to line beds with a special fleecy material. There are various commercial names for this, but, basically, it has a material backing with a soft deep fleece on the other side. It is very easy to wash and dry, and is quite hard-wearing. It allows any moisture to go through the backing, so that if your dog comes home a bit wet and goes to bed, his bedding will not get damp and he will be comfortable.

Indoor Kennels These are an excellent idea and will make your life, and the puppy's, much easier. A lot of people do not like the idea of putting their dog in a kennel, but really it is only like your bedroom, only smaller. Your Weimaraner will feel secure and safe in his, and will soon go in when he is tired. It will make house-training much easier, as your puppy will not want to mess in his bed and will tend to hang on and wait to go outside. Similarly, when he is in the kennel he cannot chew anything that he should not. If you put the puppy in the kennel when you go to the shops, he cannot get up to any mischief and you will be happy to return, knowing that your house is still in one piece. Indoor kennels are great if you are away from home, because you can take the kennel with you and be confident that your puppy will not wreck anything if he is left alone for a while. If I go away and stay in a hotel, I will take a kennel, and then I can relax, safe in the knowledge that the puppy will not chew anything or cause any damage.

The other advantage is that your dog knows that this is his bed, and he will settle much easier, even when the surroundings are strange. The indoor kennel will fold flat for storage or transportation, and you can choose one with a door in the end, the side, or both. They are usually worth their weight in gold, and worth every penny. You may decide to get one just for when your puppy is young, or, if you have the room, you may buy one big enough for an adult – it will always come in useful. It does not have to be huge; just big enough for the dog to lie with his legs straight out and tall enough for him to stand up and turn around. 24 x 27 x 30 ins (61 x 69 x 76 cms) is ideal. If you only want one for a puppy, then 24 x 24 x 24 ins (61 x 61 x 61 cms) will do.

An indoor kennel is a wise investment.

PUPPY-PROOFING

Before you collect your puppy, you need to make sure that your garden is puppy-proof. Ideally, you need to have a six-foot-high fence all around, including at the gates. If you have hedges, make sure that the puppy cannot get underneath them. A wire fence behind should make them secure, but check that there are no gaps at the bottom of the fence. Weimaraners are not dogs to wander, and you can teach them the boundaries, but you do not want to risk that with a puppy – it is better to be safe than sorry.

If you have a pond or swimming pool in your garden, make sure there is an easy exit from it in case your puppy falls in. Without a nice low way out, it has been known for puppies to drown through the exhaustion of trying to get out of the water. A piece of wood used as a ramp at one side can be all that is needed.

FINDING A VET

If you are not already registered with a veterinary surgeon, you need to find one before you bring your puppy home. Veterinary surgeries vary in the type of service that they supply to their clients. The best way to find one

that will suit your needs and expectations is to ask friends and dog owners whom they would recommend. Speak to people who you see exercising dogs in your area and ask them which vet they use, and if they are happy with them. Once you think you have found who you need, call in at the surgery to make an appointment for your puppy's first health check. If you do not like what you see or hear, then try another surgery.

As soon as possible after collecting your puppy, you should take him to your veterinary surgeon for a check-up and advice about worming and vaccinations. If there are any problems with your puppy, they can be identified immediately, and if your veterinary surgeon thinks they are detrimental to the puppy, you can still return him to the breeder before you become too attached.

COLLECTING YOUR PUPPY

When the day arrives for you to collect your puppy, take a towel and some kitchen roll with you in case there are any accidents on the way home. It is sensible to take someone with you so that one of you can keep an eye on the puppy while the other one does the driving. There is some debate about the best time of day to collect your puppy, but it is nicer for him to be introduced to his new home in the daylight, giving him time to get used to his new surroundings before he goes to bed.

Listen carefully to what your breeder tells you about your puppy. It can be a good idea to make a list of any questions you want to ask beforehand, because, in the excitement of the occasion, you will probably forget some of them! Your breeder will tell you how many times a day the puppy has been fed, what he has been fed on, when he was last wormed, etc. He will give you a diet sheet, and probably some of the food to take home for your puppy. An experienced breeder will have found out which food suits their dogs best, so unless your veterinary surgeon has any misgivings about your puppy's diet, it is as well to continue feeding the same type of food. This will reduce the chances of your puppy having an upset stomach. You will be given a pedigree and, usually, registration documents from your national Kennel Club.

THE JOURNEY HOME

For your puppy's first journey, it is often less upsetting if he is carried on someone's lap, but this can create problems in the future if it is continued for a few weeks, because he will come to expect it. If he is put in the back of a car when he is a fully-grown adult, he may bark for your attention. However, I do often think that it would be kinder to hold the puppy on your lap for the first journey, but not after that. It is

Recruit an adult to look after the puppy on the journey home.

rarely necessary to stop on the journey home to let the puppy relieve himself, as he will probably settle down on your lap and sleep. But if your journey is very long, or if he has been restless, find a quiet spot away from any houses and dogs and see if he needs to relieve himself. By letting your puppy stop and go to the toilet in a public place, you are putting the puppy at high risk, as he will not have had a vaccination and may be susceptible to catching a serious disease. The best advice is to stop for yourself if you need to, but leave the puppy in the car with someone to look after him.

SETTLING IN

Once home, give your puppy a chance to relieve himself in your garden and then offer him a drink of water before allowing him to explore his new home. Avoid the temptation to invite the whole of the neighbourhood round to admire your puppy. Give him a chance to settle in, then introduce him to your family. As he begins to feel at home, then you can offer him his first meal. Do not be tempted to add extras to his meal if he does not eat it immediately.

Weimaraners are not a food-orientated breed and would rather explore their surroundings. It is quite usual for a puppy not to eat very well for a few days, but, as long as he is playing and drinking with no vomiting or diarrhoea, then do not worry about his appetite. He will eat when he is hungry. If he learns that you may then add some more appealing canned food if he does not eat what you first give him, you are making a rod for your own back. At the next mealtime, he will expect the same treatment. The food that your breeder and veterinary surgeon have recommended is the best for your dog. He may prefer what you are eating, but that will not be as balanced as his own food, and may cause some health problems. Be firm, put his food down for ten minutes, and if he does not eat it, take it up and give it to him for his next meal. Do not give him anything else to eat. He will soon realise that, if he does not eat, he will be hungry! Weimaraners are very quick to learn, and, although your bundle of ears, legs and velvety skin may look innocent, he is capable of learning and will learn quickly.

SLEEPING

You need to decide where your

Give the puppy a chance to explore his new surroundings.

puppy is going to sleep. If you want your dog in the bedroom, then that is okay, but you cannot let him sleep in the bedroom for a few days and then put him in the kitchen. He will create havoc, because, as far he is concerned, his place is with you. If you start with him downstairs, the kitchen is ideal. He will learn that that is where he spends his nights, and soon settle. For a few nights he may create some noise, but if you ignore him, he will quickly settle down and be quiet.

When you put him to bed on the first night, if possible, have a small light on and some quiet music. He will be a bit confused for a while because he has always had his littermates for company, but he will soon settle when he is used to being on his own. If he does bark, try to avoid going back to him. If you must, go back and reassure him and then leave him. If he continues to bark, return to him but make a lot of noise, bang a tray on the table – let him know that you are not amused. If he knows that, if he cries, something nasty happens around him, then he will learn not to bark. If you go back to him when he is barking and cuddle him, he will learn that barking gets attention.

I advise that you have a bottle of wine to drink on his first night, and then you will not hear him barking! However, your neighbours might, so it is a good idea to warn them that you are getting a puppy and ask them to be patient for a couple of nights until your puppy is settled. If you have bought an indoor kennel, you will find that he will settle quickly and should not soil overnight. When you come down in the morning, greet your puppy and take him straight out. If he has soiled in the house, ignore it, as your puppy will not realise that he has made the mess and will not understand why you are cross.

FEEDING

Your puppy should be on four meals a day until he is 12 weeks old. Then, miss out his last feed so he is on three meals until he is six months old. After that, he should go on to two meals a day.

It is very important that your puppy has a balanced diet during his rapid growth stages. Do not worry about overfeeding your puppy; it is very difficult to do, because they are growing so quickly they need as much food as they can eat.

It is vital that you feed the

correct ratio of calcium (Ca), phosphorus (P), carbohydrates, protein, fat, vitamins and minerals. The easiest way to make sure you are feeding the right diet is to use one from a well-known pet food manufacturer. I find that my dogs do best on one of the top-quality premium foods. They are not cheap, but they are well worth it, because they give your dog the right diet to produce strong healthy bones, good muscles, skin condition and vitality. If you feed a balanced diet, you should not add any extra meat, vitamins or cod-liver oil, because then you are making the food unbalanced,

which can cause problems in bone development. Quite a few Weimaraners can get diarrhoea if the food contains soya or gluten. Weimaraners are prone to intolerance to these ingredients, which tend to be found in the cheaper dog foods. Your puppy does not need milk to drink – in fact, this can lead to loose stools and diarrhoea. Fresh, clean water should be provided at all times.

HOUSE RULES
Set down your house rules on day one. If you do not want him to sit on the chairs, or to go upstairs, then do not allow him to from the

Your puppy will need four meals a day until he is 12 weeks old.

It is important that 'house rules' are established.

start. Once a Weimaraner has done something once, he thinks he should always be able to do it. Similarly, if you ask him to do something, make sure it happens. If he knows that what you say will happen, he will not question you, but will do what you ask of him. If, on the other hand, you ask him to do something, and then think, 'oh it does not matter', then he will learn that you do not mean what you say and will not listen to you. Training a Weimaraner is a battle of wills – a mental challenge, not a physical one. Physically chastising a puppy will get you nowhere. If you do need to tell your puppy off (and you will), the best way is to dominate him with eye contact. Hold him from the front, with a hand on each side of his neck, and look into his eyes. He will understand that he is in the wrong, and will look away. Eye contact is very effective! If you need to be more dominant, you can roll your puppy on his back so that he is in the submissive position, but this is rarely needed if you start off on the right foot.

HOUSE-TRAINING

House-training can be done quite quickly if you are careful and watch your puppy closely for the first two days. If you catch him having an accident in the house, tell him off and go outside with him. He will forget what he is doing and it may take some time until he feels the urge to go again, but when he does, praise him. Have a word or phrase to use when you want him to go to the toilet or whenever you see him going, such as 'be clean' or 'quick' – any word will do. Once he associates the word with the action, he will perform for you on command.

Once the puppy has realised that his toilet area is outside, he will soon ask to go out when he needs to go. However, if you let him mess in the house too often, he will think that that is where he should go, and it can take a long time to get him out of the habit. It is well worth being very vigilant over the first few weeks so that you can catch him before he has an accident.

Your puppy will tend to want to go to the toilet when he has woken up and after he has been fed, and you will start to notice his distracted walk when he feels the need to go. All these are your calls to take him outside.

It is no use putting him out and shutting the door – he will think he has done something wrong. You have to go and stand out with him and wait until he goes. This may take some time, because, when he goes outside, he will forget why he is there and begin to sniff around.

This is when it is a great advantage if he links the words you are using to encourage him to go while he feels the need.

Do not be cross with him if you come home to find an accident – he will not link the punishment with his accident. However, if you catch him messing in the house, chastise him; similarly, praise him when he goes where you want him to go.

LEAD TRAINING

It is as well to start lead training well before you need to use the lead outside. As soon as your puppy comes home, get him used to his collar. Pop it round his neck, not too tightly, and then distract him so that he forgets that it is there. He will soon accept the collar as part of him.

When he is happy with his collar, attach the lead to it and let him walk around with the lead dragging behind. Once he is settled with that, you can pick the lead up without applying any pressure. Follow your puppy, so he gets used to the feeling that someone is attached to him. Then, call his name and give a gentle tug on the lead. Do not keep pulling, as he will resent it. Take your time over this. If you continue to pull on his lead he will drag his heels in and fight it with all his strength and determination. Gradually, he will learn to follow the gentle tug of the lead, especially if he gets lots of praise for doing so.

Soon your puppy will be one of the family.

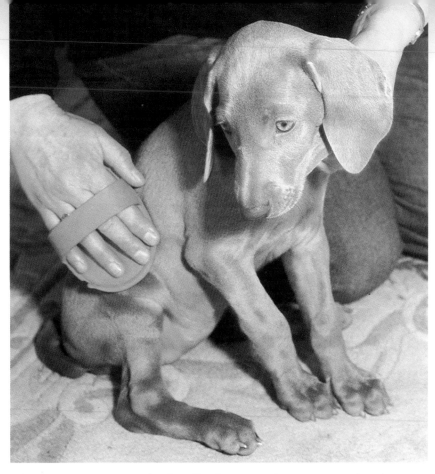

Your puppy must get used to handling from an early age, so try a few short grooming sessions.

WORMING

Most puppies are born with an infestation of roundworm, so it is essential that they are wormed from three weeks of age. Normally, they should be wormed every month until they are six months of age, and then wormed regularly thereafter. You should go to your veterinary surgeon, where they will be able to supply you with an effective and safe worming preparation and dosage details.

Tapeworm in dogs can be transferred to the dog by eating an infected flea, or infected raw offal. Segments of the tapeworm are passed from the rectum and they are flat creamy-white at first, and then dry and look like grains of rice. They can be seen on faeces or around the rectum. The best prevention for tapeworms is to make sure your dog has no fleas, and to feed him a cooked diet. Treatment should be obtained from your veterinary surgery, not a pet shop. Heartworms can be a problem in the USA, and dogs should be treated as a preventative measure before signs of infection are seen.

VACCINATION

Puppies need to be vaccinated to protect them against a range of infectious diseases. In the UK, this includes distemper, leptospirosis, hepatitis, parainfluenza and parvovirus. In some countries, your puppy will also need to be immunised against rabies. Normally, the puppy will have two injections with a minimum of two weeks between them. The usual course is started at eight weeks and completed at 12 weeks – the second injection cannot be given until then to ensure protection. Ten days after the second injection the puppy can go out on to public ground. Your puppy is safe to play with other dogs that you know are healthy and vaccinated before he has completed his full course of vaccinations. This is good socialisation for your puppy, and should be encouraged.

EARLY SOCIALISATION

Early socialisation is beneficial to your young Weimaraner's development and future temperament. Quite a few veterinary surgeries now hold puppy parties. These are arranged for puppies to come to the surgery socially, and it gives the surgery a chance to see how the puppy is developing. You can ask any questions about your puppy's development, and the puppies have a wonderful time.

Your puppy cannot go for walks until he has had all his vaccinations, but you can take him in the car and drive up the main street. This will allow him to see lots of people, lorries, buses and cars. When he is old enough to go out for walks, he will not be as shocked, as he will already have experienced the outside world.

4 Caring For Your Weimaraner

W hen you become the owner of a Weimaraner, he will rely on you to provide him with all he requires – suitable food, health care, exercise and a good home. You owe it to him to take every care to look after him in the best possible way.

FEEDING

There are many different ways to feed your Weimaraner. For an adult, I prefer to feed two meals a day; this gives your dog a more even supply of calories and it is not quite as stressful on the stomach as if you only fed once. Dogs are not like humans, and they do better if fed the same meal every day. Changes in the type of food you give can lead to diarrhoea.

COMPLETE FOODS

When you feed a complete food, dry or canned, be cautious of the manufacturer's recommended quantities to feed. As I said earlier, it is difficult to overfeed a growing Weimaraner puppy, but you can run into problems as they get older. A fat dog is not a healthy dog, and his quality of life will be lowered. When your puppy gets to six months, have a look at him – you should be able to see his last rib and notice a waist. If you cannot, you should cut his food down a bit. If he looks thin, then try to increase the amount of food he is eating. The manufacturer's job is to sell you as much food as possible, so gauge your dog's food intake by his body condition, not what it says on the label. If you are not sure that he is at the correct weight, have a chat with your vet. Most of the commercial feeds provide diets for a puppy, junior, active dog, adult dog and less active lifestyles. Ask your vet if you are unsure which diet your dog should be on.

Dry Foods: Complete foods are usually fed in a dry form and they provide a balanced diet for your dog. They can come in flake, biscuit or pellet form, and they contain all the vitamins, minerals, protein, fats and carbohydrates that your dog requires. They vary in contents, some being cereal-based, whereas the more expensive top-of-the-range brands are based on chicken and rice. As a general rule, most Weimaraners do better on the more expensive complete foods. The cheaper versions tend to contain soya and wheat gluten, which is often a cause of diarrhoea or colitis in Weimaraners.

These foods can be fed dry or soaked in water. Dry feeding is preferable, as it is better for your dog's teeth. When dogs eat, crunchy food helps to clean their teeth. It is essential that you provide plenty of fresh drinking water at all times.

Canned Foods: These types of food can be fed on their own, but are usually mixed with mixer biscuit. The cans contain lots of water and tend to be a more expensive way to feed your dog. The quality of the contents of the can is usually reflected in the price. Once again, all the essential components of the diet have been provided by the manufacturers, and no supplements are required.

FRESH MEAT
You can feed your dog on fresh meat and biscuit if you wish, but you will have to add a good vitamin and mineral supplement to make sure that he gets enough of what he needs. It is harder to feed a balanced diet because you cannot guarantee the protein: calcium: phosphorus ratios of your feed. It is preferable to use a manufactured balanced diet for your Weimaraner, especially as a puppy, when the contents of the diet are so important. I would recommend that you let the manufacturers of the food spend lots of time and money to make sure they are producing a properly balanced diet, rather than risk your own unproved recipe on your own dog.

FEEDING TIPS
- Once you find a food that suits you and your dog, stick to it.
- Leave the food down for ten minutes, then remove it until the next feed.
- Do not add any supplements to a complete food. Feed according to your dog's condition, and

It is good discipline to make your Weimaraner sit and wait before giving food.

Once you have given the food, allow your Weimaraner to eat without being distracted.

remember – fit not fat!

- Do not exercise for 30 minutes before and after feeding.
- Use a metal feeding bowl.
- If your dog has an easily-upset stomach, feed him chicken and boiled rice and then try a different type of food.
- Leave him to eat on his own. Do not stand and watch him, as he will get distracted and become fussy.
- Do not add extras to his food to encourage him to eat. He will eat when he is hungry.

DENTAL CARE

Dogs are very prone to developing dental problems. This is mainly because their teeth do not do the ripping and chewing that they were designed for.

You should start brushing your dog's teeth on a daily basis. You should not use human toothpaste as this can cause upset stomachs. There are special dog toothpastes that are flavoured to allow him to enjoy tooth brushing. You can use a human soft brush, but the specially angled canine brushes are

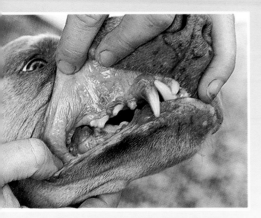

Tartar has been allowed to accumulate on the teeth.

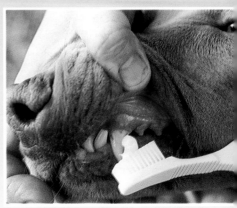

Regular brushing, or the provision of dental chews, will keep the teeth clean.

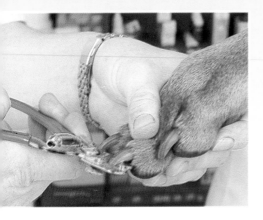

Take care not to cut into the quick of the nail.

Nails after trimming.

much more efficient and easier to use. If you do not clean his teeth, he will develop tartar on them. Tartar is a very hard substance that not only discolours the teeth near the gum, but also causes inflammation of the gums, called gingivitis. If a dog has gingivitis, the gums and teeth become infected and this will cause bad breath, pain, receding gums and, eventually, loss of teeth.

As well as brushing your Weimaraner's teeth, you can help to look after them by encouraging him to chew. Bones are excellent, but they can cause all sorts of dangerous and painful complications, so I would never give a dog any type of fresh bone. Your veterinary surgeon or pet store will have lots of toys and treated bones specifically designed to help clean your dog's teeth. Ask your vet for advice.

If your dog's teeth do become covered in tartar, he will be given a general anaesthetic by your veterinary surgeon and have the tartar removed with an ultrasonic descaler, and then the teeth will be polished. If you brush your dog's teeth, you will decrease the chances of him needing this type of treatment.

NAIL CARE

If your dog does not receive lots of exercise on hard surfaces, he will probably need his nails trimming. If you are not sure what to do, take him to your veterinary practice so that you can be shown how to do it. In the centre of the nail there is a sensitive part, the quick, which contains blood and nerves. If you cut into this, it will be painful and your dog will not be happy with any more chiropody work!

The best way to trim the nails is little and often. I would recommend that, after you have cut his nails, you give him a tidbit so that he thinks it is a fun activity.

EARS

Weimaraners can suffer from excess wax in their ears. Some wax is normal; do not worry if your dog has waxy ears if he is not bothered by them. If his ears are sore, he will shake or scratch his ears and they will be red on the inside. If this happens, you should go to your vet for treatment. There are various treatments which can be used on sore ears (otitis externa), and the sooner they are treated, the less permanent damage is done. If you do have to clean your dog's ears out, use a cleaning preparation from your veterinary surgery, and only wipe away what you can see. Do not attempt to clean deep down because you are likely to make it worse. If you use a good cleaner, it will loosen any wax and allow it to flow out on its own, preventing any chance of an infection becoming established.

Because Weimaraners have long ears with very little hair on them to protect them, they are quite prone to cutting the tips of their ears. When they do this they tend to bleed excessively. As a scab forms on the end, your dog will shake his head and knock the scab off, splattering blood everywhere! A small nick can be covered with a small plaster, but if that does not work, cut the foot out of a sock and place the leg part over the head and ears to try to stop the dog shaking them. Do not leave the ear bandaged in this way for more than 12 hours. If that does not help, you will probably require veterinary help.

EXERCISE

The Weimaraner is a gundog, bred to work on a shoot all day long. Because of this, he does require daily exercise. There is no correct amount of exercise, but, as a rough guide, you should provide him with at least a one-hour walk, allowing the majority of time for him to run free. His exercise should be gradually increased so that he can develop the muscles that he needs. Weimaraners have an excellent sense of smell and natural hunting ability, so it is best to let them exercise in an area where they can investigate the surroundings. Woods and fields have a much more interesting smell than a flat park or playing field.

When you exercise your Weimaraner, make sure you do not let him annoy other dogs and their owners. I always recommend that you put your puppy or adult on a lead when you see other dogs and people. If the other dog is friendly, then you can let them play. One of my young puppies was approached by a friendly-looking dog who then bit him. He never forgot that incident, and, like any Weimaraner, he remembered, and was always wary of other dogs after that. If I had been more careful and not allowed him to be bitten, he would not have been scared of other dogs throughout his life. He and I would have enjoyed our walks more, and would not always have been on the lookout for potential nasty dogs.

It is a good idea to let your dog do some road walking, which will keep his nails nice and short, as well as getting him used to lots of people if you go down a busy high street or market place. However, you should always be aware of any potential dangers where you walk. Even the best-trained dog should not be walked off the lead on a pavement (sidewalk) near a road. This is because, if something caught his attention on the other side, he may decide to investigate and an accident could happen. Similarly, if you are walking on a cliff ledge, or around a steep drop, be careful, as your dog may not know about the drop. It is a good idea to teach your dog to jump over walls only when you ask him. I have known too many dogs that have jumped over an innocent-looking wall, only to find that there is a huge drop on the other side.

Do not let young people take your Weimaraner for a walk, as they may not be strong enough or responsible enough to look after him. I had a phone call from a distraught family after their bitch was killed on the road when their 12-year-old daughter had taken her for a walk on the lead. As they passed a house, a dog came at the gate, barked and scared the Weimaraner. She pulled away and veered into the path of an oncoming lorry. Luckily, the lead was ripped from the girl's hand, or she may have been killed too.

When you are out on a walk with your young dog off the lead, you should periodically call your dog back to you and sometimes

The active Weimaraner requires a routine of regular exercise.

put him on the lead for a short time. If you only put him on the lead at the end of the walk, he will learn that the lead means the end of the walk and as a result may be reluctant to come back to you. If you put him on the lead for a short time and then let him off again, he will be more likely to come back to you when you call his name.

When you go for a walk in any public area, do take some plastic bags with you. It is very important that you clean up any faeces that your dog may leave so that the environment is kept clean and dogs are continued to be allowed in these areas. You can buy special bags for the purpose, but old plastic bags can be just as good.

It is important to train your Weimaraner to travel safely in the rear of the car.

CAR TRAVEL

The best place for your dog is behind a secure dog guard in an estate car, or on the back seat of a saloon car. For safety's sake, if he does travel on the seat, it is now possible to buy a harness that can be put on your dog and attached to the seat belt. This will protect him if you do have a car accident.

CHILDREN

I would never allow children to be

Think very carefully before you get involved in the business of breeding dogs.

left alone with a dog – you do not know what the children might get up to. If a group of children is playing, it is often sensible to pop the dog in his indoor kennel. This gives him a chance to rest, and also he will not become hurt or excited. As children get excited, they tend to scream in high-pitched voices, and it has been known for a Weimaraner to misinterpret these cries as those of fear and to protect 'his' child from the others. It is not the Weimaraner's fault, he is just protecting the family – he is very much a person-orientated dog.

BREEDING PRINCIPLES

Breeding a litter of puppies can be a wonderful experience, but it is also a great responsibility. Before you consider the possibility of breeding, you should consult a specialist book on the topic. There are very many important things to consider before taking the risk of producing your first litter.

SPAYING

Bitches will normally start having seasons (being 'on heat') from six to nine months of age. Some will not start until they are nearly two years of age. This is quite normal.

A bitch's season usually lasts for approximately 21 days. The beginning of the season is seen when her vulva becomes swollen and there is a bloodstained discharge. When this starts, you should keep her away from any

51

Bitches are prone to mood swings when they are in season.

male dogs and only exercise her in isolated areas, where there are no dogs. It is during the second half of her season when she will normally accept a male and allow him to mate her.

It is not a good idea to have a litter from a bitch. It does not mature her, calm her down or fulfil her. It is quite advisable and better for the bitch if you have her spayed to stop her having seasons. If you have her spayed before her first season, it is almost impossible for her to have mammary cancer when she is older. This is the biggest cancer killer in dogs. Most bitches have mood swings around their seasons and can think they are having puppies, making them quite miserable and off their food. If they are spayed, you can save them all this. Unspayed older bitches can develop an infection in the womb, which, if not surgically removed, will cause their death. This is called pyometra. The final reason for spaying is that there is no risk of an unplanned litter.

The disadvantage of spaying is that it is a major operation, although very routine. Bitches can then be more prone to put on weight (but only if overfed), and, occasionally, they can develop urinary incontinence. This can usually be treated successfully. I feel the advantages of spaying far outweigh the disadvantages.

CASTRATING

Males become sexually mature at around nine months of age and are then capable of mating. It is not a good idea to allow your dog to do this, unless he is going to be a stud dog – there is a lot to be said for 'what he does not know he cannot miss'. Once he has mated one bitch, he might well be more likely to try to find another. For a dog to become a stud dog, he must have proved himself to be an outstanding specimen of and asset to the breed. There is no point in using a mediocre dog to mate a bitch. The breed will only maintain its outstanding quality by using dogs that have shown that they are outstanding. Your pet at home might well be an excellent dog, but if he has not proved this in some kind of competition, no one will want to use him. If he is a pet and does start to become a handful, it is worth asking your veterinary surgeon whether he thinks your dog will be happier if he is castrated. A lot of male dogs are nicer pets if they are castrated.

THE VETERAN WEIMARANER

As your dog grows older, his dietary needs change. He will not be as active as he was when he was younger, and so does not require such a high number of calories in his food. Protein is still important to maintain his muscles

Neutering is a sensible option for the companion dog.

53

and body – white meat and fish are the best source. It is also necessary to provide the right amount of vitamins and minerals. Essential fatty acids in the diet, like those found in olive and cod-liver oil, will help to ease pain and inflammation in any arthritic joint.

The easiest way to provide the correct diet for the older Weimaraner is to give a good-quality proprietary senior dog food which is especially formulated to give him the greatest benefit. Any dog over eight years old could benefit from such a diet.

Most older dogs will have some degree of arthritis and muscle stiffness. This might show as a slight stiffness when getting up or an inability to jump into the car, or even, in some cases, a distinct limp. There are lots of useful treatments for arthritis and pain in dogs – anti-inflammatory drugs, pain-killers, magnetic collars, cod-liver oil, olive oil, and new treatments being developed all the time. If you think your dog may be in some pain, do go to your vet to ask about the best way to relieve it.

Regular and consistent exercise will keep your dog's muscles fit and firm, which will help to protect his joints from too much damage, and, hence, less arthritic pain. Two to three short walks every day is far better than irregular long walks. Be extra careful that he does not overdo it at the weekend when all the family are home – too much exercise that he is not used to will leave him very stiff and sore the next day.

It can be a good idea to have annual blood tests as your dog becomes older, because these may show early signs of illness before anything becomes clinically or externally obvious. Ask your vet when you take your dog for his yearly booster injections.

5 *Training Your Weimaraner*

Y ou should start training your Weimaraner as soon as your puppy comes home. The first words he must learn are his name and "No". It is the tone of your voice that will have the biggest influence on your dog. A high-pitched, happy sound is praise to a dog, but a deep, stern voice is a command. "No" means stop whatever you are doing. It is no good saying to your puppy, "Do not chew my Persian rug as it cost a lot of money" – he will not understand, but if you say "No!" to him, then this will have a much better effect! You need to use a firm voice; the tone of your voice means as much to your Weimaraner as what you say.

The important thing with a Weimaraner is to mean what you say and to make it happen. If he knows that you mean what you say, he will never challenge you, but will obey without question. He wants a pack leader – someone

The intelligent Weimaraner needs the mental stimulation that comes from training.

to look up to. You do not need to be a wonder-person to achieve this – just follow through your

Command your dog to "Wait".

Call your dog, giving lots of encouragement.

Praise your dog when the exercise is completed.

commands, as a Weimaraner never forgets.

Keep your commands consistent. It is important that everyone who takes him out for walks or trains him uses the same commands. If one person says "Sit" and then "Down" to mean 'lie flat', your dog will be confused if another person says "Sit down" – do you mean sit or lie down?

COME

When your puppy is coming towards you, call his name and hold your arms out wide apart. When he runs into your arms, praise him and he will soon get the idea.

It is a good idea to start at an early age with a gundog whistle, which can be purchased from some pet stores and all gun shops. I use two sharp pips on the whistle for the recall command. If your dog will not come to you, try running away in the opposite direction. Never chase him as he will think it is a good game and will continue to play 'catch me if you can!' If running away does not do the trick, try using a tidbit to encourage him back to you, and, if that fails, try falling on the ground and making a lot of noise or sit with your back to him. Your dog will come to you to see what you are doing, but whatever you do, *do not* chastise him when he finally comes to you. If he knows that, when he comes to you, you will tell him off, he will never come back to you. Even if you have been trying to get him to come back to you for a couple of hours, you must be nice to him and praise him, however hard this may seem.

SIT

You can start this training quite easily by letting your puppy sit before feeding him. Gently lift his head up with a hand under his chin and press firmly on his hindquarters, telling him to "Sit". He has no option but to do so. Tell him he is a good boy and let him go to the food. Do not fall into the trap of repeating "Sit, Sit, Sit", as he will learn that he does not have to obey on the first command, but on the last one. Ask him once, then make him do it!

It is a good idea to make your puppy sit at a distance away from you. Start by sitting him by your side, hold your hand up like a police officer stopping traffic, ask him to sit, and blow your whistle once. Gradually make the distance

between you and your dog greater, until he will sit when you raise your hand, pip the whistle or give the vocal command at any distance. This training is essential for gundog work, Working Trials and Obedience, but it is also invaluable for the pet. If you can sit your dog at any distance, you can stop him running across the road, chasing a cat or jumping a wall with a deep drop at the other side.

Quite a lot of show people say that you should not train a show dog to sit, because, as the judge goes over the dog and runs his hands down his back, the dog will think that he should be sitting. I do not agree with this, as when you teach your dog to stand for the judge, you should give him the command to stand. So, when the judge does touch your dog, tell him to stand. Your dog will soon learn that "Sit" means sit and "Stand" means stand.

DOWN

It is useful to get your dog to lie down. This is best taught when he is a puppy, because it can be quite difficult to manhandle an adult to the ground when he does not want you to! First, try making him sit, pat the ground in front of

STATIONARY EXERCISES

THE SIT

If necessary, apply gentle pressure on the hindquarters to coax your dog to sit.

THE DOWN

Start from the Sit position, command "Down", tapping the ground in front of the dog.

If needed, apply gentle pressure to the shoulders, and guide the front feet into position.

you, and ask him to go "Down". If this does not work, start at the sit position, gently pressing on the shoulders at the same time as holding the furthest front leg from you and pulling towards you. Tell your dog to go "Down", and he has no option but to go down. Hold him down by pressing across the shoulders. Praise him when he has done his task, and, when you have finished, make sure you tell him you have finished and praise him again.

WAIT

This command means that your Weimaraner will stay wherever he is until you have given him another command. The easiest way is, again, at mealtimes. Make him sit and tell him to "Wait" as you put his food down. Repeat the command a few times, and then tell him to get his food. Gradually increase the time, until he will wait patiently for as long as you require. If he is older when you start to train him, make him sit and keep the lead on or hold on to his collar. Tell him to "Wait" and stand directly in front of him. Make sure you do not pull on his lead. Do not use his name, because he will associate that with coming to you. If he remains

seated, take a step or two backwards and ask him to come to you. As you do this, pull his lead towards you and call his name. You can take a few steps backwards to give him room to come towards you. Praise him, and, if possible, make him sit in front of you – but the important bit is that he comes to you. This will teach him to wait, and also the first part of a simple recall. As he begins to get the idea, you can slowly increase the time and distance that you ask him to wait. If he breaks the wait, put him back in the same position and make him do it properly. Always end with a good exercise.

STAY

Stay means that the dog should stay where he is until you come back to him. Start in the same way as for the "Wait" command, only this time, ask him to "Stay". Once he has stayed in the same position, you should then return to his side before you praise him. Do not ask him to stay and then call him to you, as you will only confuse him.

HEEL

Your puppy needs to learn to walk quietly at your side on a lead. Start with your dog sitting by the

The aim in heelwork is to train your dog to walk alongside you on a loose lead, neither pulling in front nor dragging behind.

tell him to "Heel", and pull him back to your knee. Immediately release your hand from the lead. He will eventually get the idea!

RETRIEVING

One of a Weimaraner's talents is that he loves to carry things in his mouth, and you can encourage him by throwing a suitable article and telling him "Fetch". To start with, do not make him wait for his retrieve – throw it and send him for it straight away. As soon as he has picked it up, call him back to you and praise him. If he does not bring it back to you straight away, try running off in the other direction to encourage him to come back to you. Do not take the object out of his mouth straight away; praise him and wait for him to give it back to you in his own time.

BASIC TRAINING OBJECTIVES

You now have a dog who will walk quietly at heel, come to you when called, sit for his food and stay while you tie up your shoelace. It is well worthwhile putting a bit of time into training while your Weimaraner is young – it will pay dividends later. Do not be tempted to train your puppy for an hour every day, as, in the

side of your left knee. Hold the lead in your right hand, and use your left hand to tap your leg, and as you walk off, leading with your left leg, call your dog's name and tell him to "Heel". You can keep his attention with your free hand. If he pulls ahead of you, take hold of the lead with your free hand, end, he will get bored. Five minutes daily is more than enough. Be kind, consistent and determined, and you will have a dog that you can be proud of.

SPECIALIST TRAINING

It is an excellent idea to take your puppy to dog training lessons as soon as he is old enough. The classes not only train your dog, but also you, and they provide excellent socialisation. If you intend to do any gundog work, Obedience, Agility, or Working Trials, try and find a class which specialises in that particular field. Having said that, a good basic Obedience course will give you an excellent foundation.

FIELD TRIALS

The Weimaraner is expected to Hunt, Point and Retrieve. To train a dog to do all this and to wait between them takes quite a bit of time, patience and knowledge. If you intend to work or trial your dog, it is as well to go to specialist training classes. Field Trials are held to assess the quality of the work that your Weimaraner is doing.

Field Trials are organised to reflect a proper shoot day. The dogs are run on their own and must show their hunting ability and be steady if they go on point, not making the bird fly until told to do so. They then have to tenderly retrieve the shot bird and show that they can swim. It might sound easy, but it is not. However, it is thrilling when all these skills are put together and the dog works in the way that he was bred to do.

WORKING TRIALS

This kind of work involves some Obedience, retrieving articles from a 15-metre square, tracking and some jumping obstacles. The dogs love it, and there is always some good fun for both the dog and handler. The Weimaraner is well suited to this type of work.

OBEDIENCE

Obedience is not the Weimaraner's strongest point. Dogs are expected to do perfect heelwork, sits and stays, etc., and the Weimaraner is not good at it. They do not like repetitive work. Some breeds thrive on repetition and will repeat the same task at every request. However, a Weimaraner will only do the same task a certain number of times before he gets bored. By all means have a go, but it would be a real challenge!

THE RETRIEVE

With minor modifications, the same training principles apply for an Obedience Retrieve, and the Retrieve needed for a working gundog.

1. Command your dog to "Wait".

2. The dog must remain in the Sit while the dummy is thrown.

3. On command, the dog runs out to retrieve the dummy.

4. Holding, the dummy, the dog is recalled to the handler.

5. *The working gundog must learn to sit and hold the dummy. In Obedience competition, the dog would be required to come in close to the handler to present the dummy.*

AGILITY

Weimaraners love Agility. The aim is to get your dog around a course of jumps, tunnels and bending poles in the fastest time. It is an up-and-coming activity and always seems to be a lot of fun. You should not train your dog to jump over the Agility hurdles until he is a year old and his bones and joints are strong.

SHOWING

If you think your dog is good enough to show, then you should find a ring training class nearby where you can practise standing your dog. It can be great fun showing your dog, but like any of the dog activities, it can be time-consuming. If you have bought your puppy specifically to show, you should start ring training

The Weimaraner responds well to the challenge of Field Trials.

classes as soon as possible. Ask him to stand still and keep going until he does! Get any visitors to the house to look at his teeth and feel him all over. This will get him accustomed to what happens in the show world. Never lose your temper when training him, as he will remember and will probably not do it properly in future.

There are several newspapers and magazines that advertise all the shows. It is as well to start off with a local Open show and enjoy yourself. Whatever happens at the

A lot of training goes into preparing a dog for the show ring.

show, you are still taking home the best dog!

Whatever you do with your Weimaraner, at the end of the day he is your pet. Enjoy him even if he is not a show or working star – you will still love watching him run along a hedgerow, looking for something interesting, or retrieving your slippers.

6 Health Care

The Weimaraner is not prone to many health problems. He should be vaccinated as a puppy and then receive an annual booster, at which time your veterinary surgeon will give him a routine health check.

It is sensible to consider pet insurance for your puppy. There are numerous companies who provide this cover.

Ask your veterinary surgeon for advice. It is nice to know that you will not be faced with an unexpectedly large bill if your dog is unfortunate enough to have a road accident or to swallow a golf ball!

The services that veterinary surgeons can provide are always expanding, with new techniques and drugs becoming available, but they tend to be much more expensive, so it is advisable to let the insurance company take the risk of paying a large bill, not you.

EYE CONDITIONS

There are a few conditions that can affect a Weimaraner's eyes.

Entropion is when the eyelids roll in so that the eyelashes touch the eye, causing irritation. This needs surgical correction, and any affected dog should not be bred from. It has not been proved to be heritable, but it quite possibly is.

Ectropion is when the lower lids droop down all the time (not just when they are tired). This acts like a bag and collects dust, etc. and this can also cause irritation and conjunctivitis. If severe, it may require surgery to correct the problem.

Distichiasis is when hairs form an extra row of eyelashes on the rim of the eyes, which can rub on the surface of the eyes. If they cause a problem, they should be removed by your veterinary surgeon.

Cherry Eye: Dogs have a third eyelid, which flicks across the eye from the inner corner to the outer one. On the inside surface of this membrane there is a lymph gland, which can become swollen and everted – commonly called cherry eye. The cause is unknown, but if it does happen, it requires minor surgery to remove it.

Conjunctivitis: is an inflammation of the structures around the eye. The white part of the eye will appear red, there will be pus in the corner, and the eye will become sore. If it is only mild, you can try bathing the eye with cold tea, but, if it is severe, or your dog is uncomfortable, or there has been no improvement within 24 hours, you should visit your veterinary surgeon. Most cases will quickly respond to antibiotics, as conjunctivitis is often caused by bacteria. Dust and foreign bodies in the eye can also cause it.

KENNEL COUGH

This is not a serious disease, but can become a nuisance as it causes the dog to cough and cough and cough. Bacteria usually cause the infection, which can be prevented by twice-yearly vaccinations. The bacteria is easily passed on to other dogs when they are kept in close contact, so it is wise to have your dog vaccinated before you take him to dog shows, kennels or training classes. If your dog does catch kennel cough, treatment is with antibiotics and is usually very effective.

EXTERNAL PARASITES

Even the best-kept dog can pick up external parasites when he is outside.

FLEAS are the main problem, and are usually worse in the summer, but they can survive and breed all year round in your clean, dry and warm house! Fleas are reddish-brown in colour. They are hard to see, and often their presence can be seen by the coal dust-like droppings they can leave on the skin. They do not live on the dog all the time, so, as well as treating him, you should treat the house. The best way is to get a preparation from your vet. This will be effective and safe to use.

Sarcoptic Mange is a disease caused by a small mite on the skin that causes intense irritation. It is quite rare now, but quite a few dogs have caught mange from urban foxes. As more foxes are coming into our towns, the risk of infection is increasing. Symptoms are loss of hair, especially on the legs. It is easily treated with shampoos from your veterinary surgeon.

Ticks: are rarely found on Weimaraners. They live on the ground, and when they need a feed they will jump on to anything that moves past them in the hope that it is a sheep, which is the species they should feed from. Because the Weimaraner has short hair, the ticks are not happy on their coats and can easily be knocked off. Ticks look like oval warts, are cream to blue in colour, and at the base you should be able to see its legs. If you do find a tick on your dog, go to your veterinary surgeon, who will show you how to remove them properly. If done incorrectly, you could

leave the head in the skin, which would cause a nasty reaction.

ALLERGIC REACTIONS

Sometimes a dog will have an allergic reaction to either something he has eaten or something that has touched his skin. It usually happens in younger dogs, and they can develop swelling on the lips, nose and eyelids. The lips feel thickened and the eyes look red. It can appear very comical and it is usually not life-threatening, but it can be very itchy and so you should see your veterinary surgeon. It can become serious if the swelling extends inside the back of the mouth, where it can include the windpipe (trachea and larynx), causing difficulty in breathing. If this happens, you should seek veterinary advice immediately. Treatment is by antihistamines from your veterinary surgery.

Sometimes you can identify the cause of the allergic reaction, but often it is a complete mystery with no single agent being an obvious cause. Almost anything could cause an allergic reaction – plants, food, liquids, carpets, perfumes, etc. The list is never-ending. As most reactions are one-off, I would not worry too much as to the cause, but, if the episodes are repeated, it may be worthwhile to try to pinpoint what might have caused the problem.

HEATSTROKE
Dogs can only lose heat by panting. They have very few sweat glands, unlike humans. If they are left in a hot environment, they can develop heatstroke and can die. The most common cause is being left in a car in the sun with insufficient ventilation. A car with the windows left open an inch will *not* give the dog sufficient air to keep his body at the right temperature. *Do not leave your dog in a car* if there is any chance of the weather becoming hotter. The sun in spring and autumn can be just as dangerous as it is at the height of summer. Your Weimaraner will be safer and happier left at home.

Other potential problem area can be conservatories or greenhouses. Do make sure your dog cannot become trapped in one. Sadly, a puppy that I had sold died after being locked accidentally in a conservatory.

If your dog becomes too hot and develops heatstroke, he will become distressed and will pant rapidly in an attempt to lose heat. Treatment is aimed at quickly reducing his temperature – the best way is to remove him from the heat and to pour cool water over him until he becomes more settled. You must seek veterinary attention as soon as possible, because there are potentially serious consequences following heatstroke – the main ones being shock and enterotoxaemia, which can prove fatal.

BLOAT
Bloat is an extremely serious condition that can prove fatal if not treated quickly. Every owner of a Weimaraner should know about bloat so that action can be taken quickly if it occurs. It is not unique to the Weimaraner; it has been seen in many of the deep-chested breeds. Bloat normally occurs in dogs of around seven years of age or older, but it can occur at any age. Usually, it occurs in the few hours after feeding. The exact cause is not known, but certain factors are more likely to cause an attack.

Symptoms: Your dog is obviously uncomfortable and tends to pace up and down, trying to be sick without anything being produced. Sometimes you will get a small amount of white froth produced, but this is not always the case. As your dog tries to be sick, he inhales air, and this becomes trapped in the stomach, causing your dog to look bloated. If you tap the side of his abdomen, it will sound like a drum. He will become extremely distressed, and as the pressure on his stomach builds up, it causes problems with his breathing and heart. You must get him treated immediately. Phone your veterinary surgeon and tell him your problem. If treated promptly, the condition can usually be corrected with medicines, and passing a stomach tube, but if that fails, your dog will need major emergency surgery. Sometimes the stomach twists, and this rotation must be corrected surgically. If your dog needs surgery, it carries a high risk, but can be successful. Bloat is a real emergency and must be treated immediately.

Causes: No definite cause has been identified, but the present theory is that, for some reason, the normal motility (contractions) of the stomach stop. If you can get the stomach and intestines moving again, you are almost home. It is a wonderful thing if a dog you are treating for bloat passes wind, as you know things are getting back to normal!

There are various things that are possibly the cause. Any change to the normal routine can be a trigger. When I have been to a show, I do not feed my dogs when they get home. I feed them little and often during the day and then a slightly bigger breakfast the next day. The stress of whelping and feeding puppies may also be the reason why some bitches can get bloat after they whelp a litter of puppies, or when the litter starts to be weaned.

It is thought that, if food stays in the stomach for too long, it is more likely to cause decreased stomach motility. Large pieces of food, high-fibre food or fatty foods will take longer to pass out of the stomach. To minimise the risk, feed small pieces of food with low residue and low fat. Liquid food also passes through more quickly. It is sensible not to feed your dog and then exercise him straight away – allow him a period of time to digest his food. One

large meal may cause decreased gastric motility and hence increase the chances of bloat occurring. Always feed your Weimaraner at least twice daily.

Drinking large quantities of water at any one time can decrease gastric motility. Always make sure that water is available, so your Weimaraner can drink little and often. If he comes back from a walk and starts to drink a lot, pick up the water and let him only drink a little at a time.

By knowing about bloat, you can decrease the chance that it might occur. Most Weimaraners will never get bloat, so do not be too paranoid about it, but if you know about it, you will know what to do if your dog is the unlucky one. If your dog does have an attack of bloat, your vet may suggest a change of diet and daily use of drugs to maintain gastric motility to try to prevent any recurrences.

VOMITING

Lots of things can cause vomiting. If your dog is unwell and vomiting, you should go straight to your vet. If the dog seems bright and is only sick once or twice, it would be all right to starve him for 24 hours to see if that does the trick. If not, go to your veterinary surgery. Do not let your dog drink a lot of water if he has been sick. A large volume of water will surely make him sick again. If you think he has settled down, offer him just a dessertspoonful of water at a time. If he is not sick again, you can gradually increase the amount you allow him at any one time. When you start to reintroduce food, give it in small quantities and use something bland like fish, chicken, boiled rice or potatoes. Vomiting can be caused by food, viruses, bacteria, toxins or foreign bodies, or it can be a sign of another

disease. It is amazing what a Weimaraner can swallow. I have removed various things from dogs' stomachs, including plastic toys, rubber balls, socks and golf balls, to name but a few.

DIARRHOEA

This often follows on from vomiting, but not always. Again, many things can cause diarrhoea, but, in the Weimaraner, it is often food that sets it off. A few Weimaraners cannot tolerate wheat gluten or soya. Pork is also not well tolerated and should not be fed as a treat. The dog's digestive system is best suited to the same food every day.

If your dog has diarrhoea, you should starve him for 24 hours, and then, if he seems better, feed him on boiled rice and fish or chicken for three to four days. If at any stage he seems unwell, you should see your veterinary surgeon immediately. If your dog passes any blood or black faeces, this can be serious and again should be treated by a vet. Contrary to common belief, milk does not help with diarrhoea – in fact it will make it much worse. The lactose in cows' milk cannot be digested by the adult dog and it feeds bacteria which will cause the diarrhoea.

COLITIS
This can look like diarrhoea, except that the dog tends to suddenly need to go to the toilet, and the diarrhoea often has mucus and streaks of blood in it. Again, the most common cause is food intolerance, but it can be due to infection or stress. In a mild form, the dog's faeces may have a thin coating of mucus, looking like sausage skin. Your vet will suggest a diet change and prescribe some drugs to treat the colitis.

CUTS
Because the Weimaraner has a short coat, offering him little protection when he is out investigating, he can be prone to cuts and grazes. Barbed wire or broken glass are often the culprits.

Your course of action should depend on the size and depth of the cut.

A small oozing cut is best just bathed in salt water and allowed to heal on its own. If the cut is larger than half an inch (12mm), it will probably need veterinary attention. Cuts to the pad can be a problem. The top layers of the pad are dead tissue, and will not heal when cut. If the cut is deep and goes into the sensitive part of the pad, it may need suturing. The cut will gradually grow out of the pad as the healed part moves to the surface.

Care should be taken with deep wounds to the foot and pad, because they may look small at the surface, but the wound could involve the tendons of the foot. If they are cut, they will need repairing to allow full recovery. There is a large blood supply to the foot and cuts to this area can bleed profusely. If any cut is bleeding badly, you should apply a pressure bandage, which can be made with any material, ideally a large quantity of cotton wool (cotton) and a firmly-applied bandage. In an emergency, anything can be used – from a jumper to a tea towel. The important thing is to produce pressure on the wound that will stop the bleeding. If you cannot stop it, it may be necessary to put a temporary tourniquet on an injured limb. You can use a lead or a piece of rope to tie tightly around the limb to stop the blood supply, and hence stop the bleeding. If you do apply a tourniquet, do not leave it on for more than 15 minutes, or you can cause oxygen-starvation damage to the leg. Badly bleeding cuts should be seen by a vet after you have applied a pressure bandage.

Many cuts can become infected, particularly if caused by barbed wire or dog bites. You should seek veterinary advice especially if the wound begins to become swollen, red or discharging.

HAEMATOMAS

A haematoma is basically a bruise. They can occur all over the body, but young puppies are quite prone to getting them on the top of the head, usually when they bang their heads on hard objects like the underneath of a chair or table. Another common place is the side of the ribcage. Haematomas are painless, quite hard and can be as big as an egg. They require no treatment and will settle completely if left alone, but it can

take several months in some cases. Do check with your vet if you are worried.

LUMPS

It is easy to see lumps and bumps on your Weimaraner as he has a short coat. Many lumps are nothing to worry about, but it might be a malignant cancer, and if untreated it could cause your dog's death.

If you find any lumps, go to your veterinary surgeon for an examination. The sooner a cancer is removed, the greater the chance of a complete recovery. Breast cancer (mammary cancer) is the biggest cancer killer in dogs. If your bitch has not been spayed, she has a greater chance of developing this type of cancer. Take extra care in examining her in the two months after her season, as this is a very common time for tumours in the mammary glands to start to grow.

ANAL GLANDS

At each side of the anus, just under the skin, there are two anal glands. These should empty every time the dog passes a stool, but occasionally they do not, and as they fill up they can cause an irritation. This will cause the dog to rub his bottom on the ground, or lick around the base of the tail. If the glands are not emptied, they can become infected and can develop an abscess. It is as well to let your vet empty the glands, as it is not easy, and the contents of the gland are extremely smelly.

PYOMETRA
This is a condition that occurs in the bitch two to three months after a season. The uterus becomes full of pus and toxins, and, if left untreated, will cause death. The symptoms include excessive thirst, depression (usually), and often, a nasty vaginal discharge. It is most common in the middle-aged to old

dog. Treatment can be medical or surgical. Surgery involves the removal of the uterus and ovaries, and is often the treatment of choice unless the dog is very old and the anaesthetic would be too much, or if you want to breed from your bitch. In these cases, a series of injections might be used.

FALSE PREGNANCY

This is a normal response in a bitch following a season when she has either not been mated or she has failed to become pregnant.

The hormones in a pregnant and non-pregnant bitch follow the same pattern after a season. Some bitches are more sensitive to them than others and will show all the signs of being pregnant. Signs of false pregnancies can vary from full nesting behaviour, milk production, lack of appetite and carrying toys, or just mood changes. The signs will go away in about two weeks, but, if she is getting quite distressed, you can now treat her with a drug that will not cause any long-term side effects. Ask your veterinary surgeon for advice.

HIP DYSPLASIA

Hip dysplasia (HD) is a problem that affects the hip joint. There are several reasons why it should occur – it can be inherited or environmental, it can be caused by too much or too little exercise when young, or by incorrect feeding. The hip joint is a ball-and-socket joint and the ball should fit smoothly and quite tightly in the socket. If it does not, it is called HD, and in bad cases can lead to pain, inflammation and arthritis.

To reduce the chances of HD occurring, prospective sires and dams should be X-rayed and the films examined by the appropriate veterinary body for analysis. In the UK, a low score is indicative of well-formed hips. As HD can be due to other factors, it is important that you feed a good quality balanced food, do not give extra vitamins or minerals and exercise your puppy sensibly – too much is as bad as too little.

Hip dysplasia is not a common problem in Weimaraners.

JUVENILE PYODERMA

Also known as puppy head gland disease or strangles, this occurs in puppies of six to 16 weeks of age. The face becomes swollen and crusts form all over the head, and the puppy is sore and unhappy. Treatment is with corticosteroids and antibiotics, and, if they are administered promptly, it will produce a complete cure. If treatment is delayed it can lead to scarring on the face.

SYRINGOMYELIA

This is believed to be an inherited condition, and is seen when the puppy first starts to walk. There is a defect in the spinal cord and the puppy's gait is uncoordinated – typically producing a bunny-hop during running. There is no treatment, and although most can cope, some have to be put to sleep. It is not a common problem.